Australia

Fred Martin

Heinemann Library
Des Plaines, Illinois

Designed by AMR
Illustrations by Art Construction
Printed in Hong Kong / China

02 01 00 99 98
10 9 8 7 6 5 4 3 2 1

Library of Congress Cataloging-in-Publication Data

Martin, Fred, 1948-
    Australia / Fred Martin.
        p.   cm. — (Next stop!)
    Includes bibliographical references and index.
    Summary: Introduces the landscape, weather, plants, animals,
    products, and culture of Australia.
    ISBN 1-57572-675-0 (library binding)
    1. Australia—Juvenile literature. [1. Australia.] I. Title.
    II. Series.
    DU96.M26   1998
    994—dc21   97-53108
                                                                   CIP
                                                                    AC

Acknowledgments
The Publishers would like to thank the following for permission to reproduce photographs:
Aspect Pictures, Derek Bayes, p.25, John Earrett, p.23, Alex Langley, p.14; Colorific Photo Library,
Bill Bachman, p.6, Philip Hayson, p.26, Penny Tweedie, p.19, Barbara Wale, p.4,
David Young, p.18; J. Allan Cash, p.11; Panos Pictures, Penny Tweedie, pp.9, 27, 28; Still Pictures,
Mark Edwards, pp.15, 22, Klein/Hubert, pp.7, 8, Gerald and Margi Moss, pp.5, 10; Trip Photo
Library, R. Nichols, p.24, Eric Smith, pp.12, 13, 16, 17, 21, 29.

Cover photographs: Life File and Still Pictures

Our thanks to Betty Root for her comments in the preparation of this book.

Every effort has been made to contact holders of any material reproduced in this book.
Any omissions will be rectified in subsequent printings if notice is given to the Publisher.

Any words appearing in bold, **like this,** are explained in the Glossary.

CONTENTS

INTRODUCTION TO AUSTRALIA

AUSTRALIA'S HISTORY

Nobody knows when the first people went to Australia. It could have been 50,000 years ago. These people are called **aborigines**.

In 1780, Captain James Cook, an English explorer, landed on the east coast. He landed in a place he called Botany Bay. After that, Australia was ruled by Britain.

Aborigines painted on rocks. These are special places to the aborigines.

Australia: towns and population

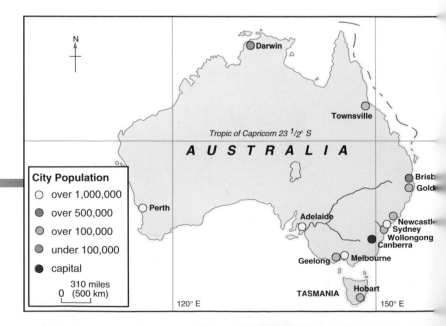

City Population
- ○ over 1,000,000
- ◔ over 500,000
- ◑ over 100,000
- ◕ under 100,000
- ● capital

310 miles
0   (500 km)

Darwin

Townsville

Tropic of Capricorn 23 1/2° S

AUSTRALIA

Perth

Adelaide

Brisb
Gold

Newcastl
Sydney
Wollongong
Canberra

Geelong   Melbourne

TASMANIA   Hobart

120° E   150° E

Captain Cook landed here in 1780. The city of Sydney grew around a small cove.

CONVICTS AND SETTLERS

In the early days, **convicts** were sent to Australia from England as a punishment. Many of them never went back. Later, people from Britain and other countries went to Australia to farm and to look for gold.

A NEW COUNTRY

In 1901, Australia became a new country with its own **government**. Over the past hundred years, many more people have moved to Australia. Now there are eighteen million people in Australia.

Australia's flag is blue with white stars. There is a seven-pointed star for the seven parts of Australia. The other stars show the Southern Cross which is a group of stars in the sky over Australia. In the corner of the flag, there is also a small Union Jack which is the British flag.

THE LAND

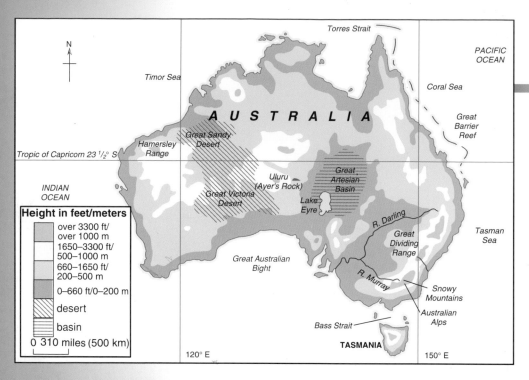

Map labels:
Torres Strait
PACIFIC OCEAN
Timor Sea
Coral Sea
Great Barrier Reef
AUSTRALIA
Great Sandy Desert
Hamersley Range
Tropic of Capricorn 23 ½° S
Uluru (Ayer's Rock)
Great Artesian Basin
INDIAN OCEAN
Great Victoria Desert
Lake Eyre
R. Darling
Tasman Sea
Great Dividing Range
Great Australian Bight
R. Murray
Snowy Mountains
Australian Alps
Bass Strait
TASMANIA
120° E
150° E

Height in feet/meters
- over 3300 ft/ over 1000 m
- 1650–3300 ft/ 500–1000 m
- 660–1650 ft/ 200–500 m
- 0–660 ft/0–200 m
- desert
- basin

0 310 miles (500 km)

Australia: natural features

A CONTINENT

Australia is too big to be called an island. It is called a **continent**. It is the smallest of the Earth's seven continents.

PLAINS AND RIVERS

Most of Australia is flat and low with some hills. There are only a few rivers because there is not much rain.

Much of Australia is lowland. Farmers use the land for cattle ranching.

UNDERGROUND WATER

There is plenty of water trapped in the rocks deep underground. It got there by trickling down through the rocks above. This water is used by farmers for their animals.

MOUNTAINS

The Snowy Mountains are along the eastern edge of Australia. The most unusual thing in the landscape is near the middle of Australia. It is called *Uluru*, or Ayer's Rock. It is a rock 1,150 feet (348 meters) high, with very steep sides. The sun makes it look different colors at different times of the day.

Lake Eyre is the biggest lake in Australia but it is empty for most of the time. The rivers that flow into it are usually dry because there is so little rain.

Uluru, or Ayer's Rock, is a giant rock that stands up from the plain in the outback. Tourists come to see Uluru.

WEATHER, PLANTS, AND ANIMALS

This is a forest with eucalyptus trees. There is not much forest left in Australia.

WET AND DRY

The middle of Australia is so hot and dry that it is a desert. The wettest places are in the north. There is rain when hot, wet air blows south from the **equator**. In the southeast, it is warm and dry in summer and it rains in the winter.

Kangaroos live in the wild in Australia's **outback**. You can see the kangaroo's pouch and the young kangaroo.

PLANTS

Only small bushes and some wild flowers grow in the deserts. Grass and some trees grow where it is wetter. There are **rain forests** where it is hot and wet.

ANIMALS

Kangaroos live in Australia. They are marsupials. This means they have a pouch for their young. A young kangaroo is called a joey. There are also koalas, wild dogs called dingoes, snakes, and poisonous spiders in Australia. Rabbits are pests because they eat grass that farmers want for their sheep and cattle.

Winter in Australia is during June, July, and August. This is because Australia is in the southern half of the world.

9

TOWNS AND CITIES

THE BIG FIVE CITIES

Almost everyone in Australia lives in a city. There are five big cities. Sydney is the biggest with almost four million people. The others with over a million people are Melbourne, Brisbane, Perth, and Adelaide.

SYDNEYSIDERS

Sydney is on the shores of a natural **harbor** called Port Jackson. Captain Cook built the first houses there in 1780. Now Sydney is Australia's biggest city and its biggest **port**. People who live there are called "Sydneysiders."

Sydney is the biggest cit in Australia. The highest buildings are in the city center.

OTHER TOWNS AND CITIES

The **capital city** of Australia is Canberra. This is where the **government** meets. Alice Springs is a town in the middle of Australia. Farmers from hundreds of miles away go there to shop. There are towns for miners near mines and quarries. One of these towns is Mount Tom Price.

Coober Pedy is a small town in the southeast of Australia. Just under half the people in Coober Pedy live in homes under the ground. This is because it is cooler under ground than it is above.

Melbourne is the second largest city in Australia. This shopping mall is in the center of the city. There are no cars in this street but people can travel by trolley.

A CITY FAMILY

The Rich family in their garden

THE RICH FAMILY

The Rich family live in St. Ives which is about twelve miles (twenty kilometers) from Sydney. Geoffrey and Jane Rich have three children. They are Graeme, aged thirteen, Katie, aged ten, and Jenna, aged six.

THE FAMILY HOME

The family lives in a big house with four bedrooms. There is a big back yard and a swimming pool. They sit under the **veranda** during the hot summer.

There are good roads and many trees in this area.

WORK, SCHOOL, AND SHOPS

Geoffrey Rich goes to work in Sydney by train every day. He works in the law courts as a lawyer. The children all go to local schools. Jenna likes reading best. Jane does most of the shopping in a supermarket in St. Ives.

ENJOYING LIFE

Everyone in the family plays a sport, such as tennis or rugby. The family often goes **bushwalking**. A favorite family vacation is to go to the beach.

Katie plays softball in the park in **St. Ives.** Her mother coaches the softball team.

There is a supermarket in **St. Ives.**

Jenna goes to an elementary school in St. Ives. Can you see when this photo was taken?

FARMING IN AUSTRALIA

OUTBACK STATIONS

The biggest farms in Australia are in the dry areas called the **outback**. Cattle and sheep are reared on these farms. These huge farms are called **stations**.

GRAZING LAND

Cattle and sheep graze on whatever grass they can find. There are no fields with fences. In very dry years, sheep and cattle can die of thirst if rivers and water holes go dry.

Sheep are reared for their wool.

Wheat is grown on some farms. Farmers use machinery to harvest the wheat.

FARM WORKERS

Stockmen on horseback or on motorcycles round up the cattle and sheep. Another way to find the animals is by helicopter. Teams of **shearers** travel around Australia shearing the wool off the sheep.

GROWING CROPS

Farmers grow crops such as wheat, cotton, and fruit. Some crops have to be watered because it is so dry. Putting water onto the fields is called **irrigation**.

There are about 130 million sheep and 22 million cattle in Australia.

A COUNTRY FAMILY

THE FAMILY FARM

The Reid family live on a farm that is 25 miles (40 kilometers) from Cowra, the nearest town. They have a large farm.

THE FARMHOUSE

The family lives in a farmhouse with a wide **veranda**. They get their water from a tank that collects rain on the roof. They have electricity for cooking, light, heat, and for the T.V.

A small part of the Reid family's farm

The family farmhouse. Can you see what the house is made of?

Chris Reid at a sheep market. The sheep are sold for their wool and meat.

INTO COWRA

The youngest children, Anna aged nine and Toby aged seven, go to school in Cowra. Libby, their mother, also works and does most of the shopping in Cowra. Two older children go away to a boarding school in Sydney.

PLAY TIME

The children have a tree house in their back yard. They go swimming in a nearby river. They enjoy living in the country where they have the whole farm to explore.

Dinnertime in the evening when the children come back from school in Cowra

Anna in her classroom

SHOPS AND SERVICES

Drivers can buy drinks from this shop without getting out of their car.

CITY SHOPS

Most Australians live in cities and do their shopping there. There are big department stores and shopping malls with smaller shops. Shops along the roads often have awnings so shoppers can walk in the shade.

CARS AND SHOPPING

Many people use cars to shop. You can drive into some shops and buy what you want without getting out of your car.

OUTBACK SHOPS

There are not many towns or shops in the **outback**. Farmers on sheep and cattle **stations** have to drive a long way to these towns. Some fly in their own small airplanes.

OUTBACK SERVICES

If someone is ill in the outback, the Flying Doctor service will visit. Some children live too far away to go to school so they listen to their teacher on a radio.

A Flying Doctor can get to anyone in the outback in no more than ninety minutes.

There is a Flying Doctor service in the Australian outback. This is because people live far way from a doctor or hospital.

AUSTRALIAN FOOD

HUNTERS

The **aborigines** used to hunt and collect all the food they needed. This food is called "bush tucker." They used spears to kill kangaroos and other animals. They also used boomerangs.

FOOD FROM EVERYWHERE

People who came from other countries have brought different food to Australia. The English cooked lamb and roast beef. Italians brought pizzas and Greeks brought kebabs. People from Asia brought rice dishes cooked in an open pan called a wok.

Cooking on a barbecue is a popular way to have a meal.

This is a Greek restaurant. Many Australian people enjoy eating food from different countries.

SPECIAL FOODS

Australians can buy kangaroo steaks in restaurants and supermarkets. Freshwater lobsters called *yabbies* are also popular. Fruits, such as pineapples and mangoes, are grown in the northeast.

A dessert called Peach Melba is named after Dame Nellie Melba. She was an Australian opera singer.

THE "BARBIE"

Because the weather is often warm, Australians like to cook over an open-air barbecue. Beef, lamb, chicken, or fish are roasted over red-hot charcoal. A barbecue is also a way to entertain friends.

MADE IN AUSTRALIA

MINING

Copper, iron, **bauxite,** and other metals are found in the rocks in Australia. Coal is burned in power stations to make electricity. Precious stones, such as opals and diamonds, are also found in the rocks.

These diggers are digging bauxite from the rocks. Mining can destroy the forests.

SACRED LAND

Some of the metals and precious stones are on sites that are **sacred** to the **aborigines**. Others are on **wilderness** land and in **rain forests** that people want to protect. People often disagree about allowing mining in these areas.

THE FOOD INDUSTRY

Many types of food are taken to factories to be processed. Sugarcane is made into sugar and grapes are crushed to make wine. Some foods, such as peaches, are put in cans.

FACTORY WORK

Cars, chemicals, electronic goods, and many other things are made in Australia. Most factories are in the big cities, including Sydney, Melbourne, and Adelaide.

More diamonds and more bauxite are mined in Australia than in any other country.

Picking grapes to make wine. The wine is made in a winery.

23

TRANSPORTATION

CITY TO CITY

Most Australian cities are hundreds of miles apart. Darwin and Perth are over 1,000 miles away (1,600 kilometers) from each other. They are even farther from Sydney.

BY TRAIN OR PLANE

You can travel far by train in Australia. The ride between Sydney and Perth takes almost three days. It only takes 4 hours and 35 minutes in an airplane.

A road train is a truck with trailers. They are used to carry cattle.

This monorail runs around the city center of Sydney. The monorail helps keep cars off the city roads.

OUTBACK DRIVING

The main roads in Australia all have good, hard surfaces. Some roads in the **outback** are only dirt tracks. They can be flooded when there is heavy rain. Drivers in the outback always take spare water and gasoline with them. It is a long way between houses and even farther between gas stations.

The world's longest stretch of straight railway line goes across the Nullarbor Plain. It is 310 miles (500 kilometers) long.

ROAD TRAINS

Trucks with trailers are called "road trains." They take cattle from cattle **stations** to the city markets.

SPORTS AND HOLIDAYS

SPORT FOR ALL

Almost half of all Australians are members of sports teams. There are teams for rugby, soccer, tennis, cricket, swimming, golf, and many other sports. Australia's rugby team is called the "Wallabies." A wallaby is a small kangaroo. Australia's golfers often compete in international competitions.

These surf boats are used by lifesavers. They are having a race to see which team of lifeguards is the best.

WARM WEATHER AND SEA

Australia's warm and dry weather makes it easy to play outdoor sports for most of the year. Swimming, surfing, and sailing are also popular. Australian yachts compete in "around the world" and other yacht races.

The Great Barrier Reef is a wall of living and dead coral. It is just over 1,250 miles (2,000 kilometers) long.

VACATIONS IN AUSTRALIA

Almost every type of vacation is available in Australia. People can snorkel and scuba dive to see coral and fish on the Great Barrier Reef. Some people prefer to visit the outback or to go **bushwalking**. There are also natural wonders to see, such as the giant rock called *Uluru* or Ayer's Rock. There is even skiing in the Australian Alps.

Some people like to go bushwalking. They camp overnight in the open.

FESTIVALS AND ARTS

ANCIENT ARTS

Australia's oldest arts and festivals come from the **aborigines**. They made paintings and carvings on rocks in **sacred** places. The aborigines also made their own musical instruments and enjoyed dancing.

This is an aborigine dance. The dancers sometimes imitate the way animals move or show how people go hunting.

FESTIVALS

New festivals were brought to Australia by people from Europe. Many of these are Christian festivals such as Easter and Christmas.

THE ARTS

There are art galleries, museums, theaters, and the movies in the cities. The Sydney Opera House is a landmark on Sydney's skyline.

MOVIES

Many movies are made in Australia. There have been some popular movies made including *Crocodile Dundee* and the *Mad Max* films. Mel Gibson and Nicole Kidman are two of Australia's well-known movie stars.

This unusual looking building is the Sydney Opera House. The roof looks like the sails on a boat.

A boat race in Alice Springs is held when the river is dry. The teams run with their boats along the river bed.

AUSTRALIA FACTFILE

People

People from Australia are called Australians.

Capital city

The **capital city** of Australia is Canberra.

Largest cities

Sydney is the largest city with nearly four million people. The second largest city is Melbourne and Perth is the third largest city.

Head of country

Australia is ruled by a prime minister and a **government**. The British Queen is the Head of State.

Population

There are over 18 million people living in Australia.

Money

The money in Australia is the Australian dollar ($A).

Language

Most people in Australia speak English, with a few others including **Aboriginal** dialects, Greek and Italian.

Religion

Most people who have religious beliefs in Australia are Christian.

GLOSSARY

aborigine the people who first lived in Australia

bauxite type of rock that contains aluminum

bushwalking walking and camping in the Australian bush

capital city the city where a country has its government

continent the largest areas of land on earth, such as Asia and Australia

convict someone who has been found guilty of a crime and is sent to prison

equator the line around the middle of the Earth

government people who run a country

harbor an area of sheltered water

irrigation to put water on fields to water plants

outback the area in the middle of Australia away from towns and the coast

port a city with docks for ships

rain forests the natural forests in hot and wet tropical areas

sacred special because of religious beliefs

shearers people who cut wool off sheep

stations the word used in Australia to describe a very large farm for sheep or cattle

stockmen men who look after the animals on a farm or station

veranda a shady area outside a house, with a large overhanging roof

wilderness remote areas with natural vegetation

INDEX

MORE BOOKS TO READ

Baily, Donna, *Australia,* Chatham, NJ: Raintree Steck-Vaughn. 1990.

Bickmann, Connie, *Children of Australia.* Minneapolis, MN: Abdo & Daughters, 1994.

Santrey, Laurence, *Australia,* Mahwah, NJ: Troll Communications. 1985.